ADRENALIN!
Snowboarding

Clive Gifford

Chrysalis Children's Books

First published in the UK in 2005 by
Chrysalis Children's Books
An imprint of the Chrysalis Books Group Plc
The Chrysalis Building, Bramley Road,
London W10 6SP

ISBN 1 84458 400 3

British Library Cataloguing in Publication Data for this book is available from the British Library.

Associate Publisher Joyce Bentley
Senior editor Rasha Elsaeed
Project editors Jon Richards and Kate Simkins
Editorial assistant Camilla Lloyd
Designer Ed Simkins
Consultant Tudor Thomas
Twice UK national snowboard champion, Tudor Thomas is editor-in-chief of
White Lines magazine, Britain's biggest and most established snowboarding publication.
He has been involved in many aspects of the sport from product testing to board graphic
design and has over 15 years of snowboarding experience.

Produced by Tall Tree Ltd, UK

Printed in China

10 9 8 7 6 5 4 3 2 1

Typography Natascha Frensch
Read Regular, READ SMALLCAPS and Read Space; European Community Design Registration 2003
and Copyright © Natascha Frensch 2001-2004 Read Medium, **Read Black** and *Read Slanted*
Copyright © Natascha Frensch 2003-2004

READ™ is a revolutionary new typeface that will enhance children's understanding through clear,
easily recognisable character shapes. With its evenly spaced and carefully designed characters,
READ™ will help children at all stages to improve their literacy skills, and is ideal for young
readers, reluctant readers and especially children with dyslexia.

Contents

Snow surfing

Every year, millions of snowboarders ride the slopes at resorts all around the world. They are taking part in the fastest-growing winter sport around, a sport that is packed with thrills and excitement and has created its own fashion, films and culture.

Why snowboard?

Once they've carved out their first few turns, the only question most new snowboarders ask is, 'why didn't I do this before?' Snowboarding is about freedom. With just the board strapped to your feet, you're free to glide, turn and move across beautiful winter scenery. Snowboarding is easy to learn and no snowboarder has ever run out of places to ride or new challenges to try. There are so many different slopes, terrains and snow types to master, as well as different moves to perfect. If that's not enough, hundreds of competitions exist at local, national and international level.

A BOARDER GLIDES EFFORTLESSLY DOWN A SLOPE THAT IS COVERED IN POWDER — A TOP LAYER OF FRESH SNOW.

Snowboarding flavas

There are a great many snowboarding styles to choose from, but the two main flavours are freeriding and freestyle. Freeriding is where you start your snowboarding career, cruising the slopes of a winter resort, making turns and moves. Experienced freeriders will seek out moguls (humps in the snow) or natural jumps in the terrain to get airborne and to perform spins and other moves. Freestyle snowboarding is the most spectacular of the main styles and is all about tricks. Freestylers aim to get big air from jumps either on slopes or on special U-shaped 'bowls' called halfpipes or quarterpipes dug into the snow.

EXPERIENCED SNOWBOARDERS SEEK OUT PRISTINE SLOPES, OFTEN IN REMOTE PLACES THAT ARE FAR FROM THE OFFICIAL ROUTES, OR PISTES.

The language of boarding

Snowboarding is full of slang. Many of the technical terms and words for tricks are at the back of the book, but here are a few of the everyday words that snowboarders use.

FLAIL	Riding badly and out of control.
JIB	A rail or anything other than snow that a board is ridden on.
KICKER	A medium-sized jump.
POSEUR/POSER	Someone who pretends to be better than they are.
SHREDDER	What snowboarders call themselves.
STEEZ	Style. Can be good (mad steez), really good (sick steez) or bad (beat steez).
TWO-PLANKER	A skier.
WACK	Something that is not good, such as ski slopes being closed or breaking your snowboard.
WIPEOUT	A major crash.

Early boarding

Snowboarding is a young sport. It began in the 1960s when American Sherman Poppen designed a toy for his two children. Poppen called his new board a Snurfer.

Early days

Poppen built his first Snurfer in 1965 for his daughter and started making them for sale in 1966. The Snurfer was designed to glide across hard snow and was steered by a rope held in the hands. Almost half a million Snurfers were sold, but it was thought of as a toy for children rather than a sport even though Poppen organised riding competitions. By the 1970s, the kids who had ridden Snurfers grew up into adults and started designing and building their own snowboards. These pioneers included Dimitrije Milovich, Tom Sims and Jake Burton Carpenter.

BOARDING FACT

Dimitrije Milovich was a surfer who worked as a waiter during the early 1970s. He used plastic cafeteria trays to slide across snow. In doing so, he invented a new type of snowboard called the Winterstick.

AN ORIGINAL WOODEN SNURFER WITH THE GUIDE ROPE FIXED TO THE NOSE. THE WORD 'SNURFER' IS A COMBINATION OF THE WORDS 'SURF' AND 'SNOW'.

The first snowboards

Jake Burton Carpenter took part in Snurfer competitions as a child. After graduating from college, he built more than 100 prototype boards, experimenting with different designs. His first snowboards came out in 1977. They were made from wood and fibreglass and had bindings for the rider's boots. Burton promoted snowboarding as a sport and founded an event at Stratton Mountain, USA, in 1982.

BOARDING PIONEER JAKE BURTON RIDING ONE OF HIS SNURFERS. WHEN HE SET UP THE BURTON COMPANY, HE HIRED TWO FAMILY MEMBERS AND A FRIEND TO HELP WITH PRODUCTION.

The big time

The competition Burton founded has grown to become the US Open, the world's greatest freestyle snowboarding event. Burton still snowboards today, along with managing his snowboard company, the largest board-makers in the world.

JAKE BURTON (RIGHT) ALONGSIDE FELLOW BOARDING PIONEER TOM SIMS.

Modern boarding

Snowboarding developed its style and equipment throughout the 1980s. Competitions and companies expanded, and the number of snowboarders rose from hundreds to almost two million by 1990.

'Bad boy' Image

Early snowboards were hard to control and, without dedicated riding areas or instructors, there were plenty of accidents. Ski resorts barred them from their slopes and by 1985, less than 10 per cent of all North American resorts allowed snowboarders. However, snowboarding rallied and more and more resorts started providing snowboarding lessons and welcoming boarders. Today, more than 90 per cent of resorts all around the world welcome snowboarding.

SNOWBOARDING IS SO POPULAR THAT IT INFLUENCES THE SKI WORLD, AS SHOWN BY THIS SKIER GETTING SOME AIR ABOVE A BOARDING HALFPIPE.

A growing sport

Snurfers and early snowboarders raced side by side at the first ever major competition in 1982 on Suicide Six Ski Hill in Vermont, USA. Tom Sims, who broke his thumb in the competition, won the World Snowboarding Championships the following year. It was the first contest to feature a halfpipe event. Major competitions followed in Europe in 1986 – in Livigno, Italy, and St Moritz, France. In the same year, French rider Regis Rolland starred in the first influential snowboarding video, *Apocalypse Snow*.

SOME PRO BOARDERS CASH IN ON THE POPULARITY OF BOARDING BY RELEASING VIDEOS AND OTHER PROMOTIONAL MATERIAL. THIS IMAGE IS FROM A VIDEO BY BOARD MASTER JOHAN OLOFSON.

SNOWBOARD EVENTS ATTRACT CROWDS OF THOUSANDS OF PEOPLE. THIS FREESTYLE EVENT WAS HELD IN 2000 ON AN ARTIFICIAL SLOPE CONSTRUCTED IN MANCHESTER, UK.

The 1990s

Skateboard companies like H-Street and Santa Cruz Skateboards turned to snowboarding in the early 1990s. Soon, over 50 companies were producing boards, kit and clothing. By the late 1990s, snowboarding had boomed into the world's fastest growing winter sport. More than 30 per cent of all visits to ski resorts in the USA and Canada were by snowboarders. With more than seven million snowboarders in 2000, it is predicted that snowboarders will outnumber skiers on the slopes by 2012.

The board

Hang out with snowboarders for any length of time and talk will turn to kit and clothing. There is a bewildering variety of equipment around and some of it is expensive. It is a good idea to rent kit on your first few visits to the slopes.

Freeride and freestyle

Boards come from dozens of manufacturers in many colours and designs, but there are two main types based on the two main types of riding – freeride and freestyle boards.

The stomp pad is a small pad, often made of rubber, on the deck of the board. It provides grip when riders push their boards across flat snow without their feet in the bindings.

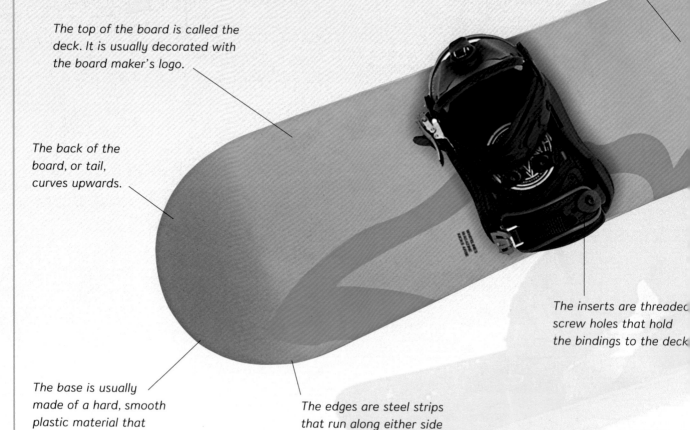

The top of the board is called the deck. It is usually decorated with the board maker's logo.

The back of the board, or tail, curves upwards.

The inserts are threaded screw holes that hold the bindings to the deck

The base is usually made of a hard, smooth plastic material that glides well over snow.

The edges are steel strips that run along either side of the board.

Beginners' decks

Freeride boards (also known as all-round or all-mountain) are the type of board most beginners use. They can be used in different snow conditions and are directional boards. This means that they are designed to be ridden in one direction and their tips are turned up more than their tails.

The bindings fit tightly to the board.

FLOW

The front of the board – called the nose or tip – curves up.

Freeride board

Jumping and twisting

Freestyle boards are usually lighter and shorter than freeride boards, making them easier to jump and twist with. They tend to be quite flexible and have similar shaped tips and tails to ride in either direction.

AS WELL AS THE STYLE OF RIDE, BOARDERS NEED TO TAKE INTO ACCOUNT THEIR HEIGHT, AGE AND WEIGHT, AS WELL AS THE CONDITIONS WHEN CHOOSING A BOARD.

Freestyle board

Dressing the part

As well as the right kind of snowboard, boarders must have the correct clothing before they hit the slopes. The mountains can be a dangerous place, and it is important to have the right kind of clothing to keep you warm.

Plenty of layers

If you keep warm and dry, you will find that your snowboarding skills hot up as well. The key is to dress in layers, with warm, insulating inner layers and a waterproof outer layer. Your clothing should fit well but allow plenty of room to move. A hat made from artificial fibres, not wool, and close-fitting snowboarding gloves are also essential gear.

SNOWBOARDING TROUSERS ARE WATERPROOF AND HAVE REINFORCED KNEES AND SEATS THAT ARE SOMETIMES PADDED.

Boarding fashion

The impact of snowboarding has carried over into the fashion world. Boarders favour loose-fitting clothing both on and off the slopes. These include trousers and T-shirts that are covered in bright patterns and snowboard company logos. Many of these garments can now be bought in shops that are far from any snow.

Foot gear

There are two types of boots – soft and hard. Most people use soft boots that are more flexible. Boarders who enter racing competitions tend to prefer hard boots that have a plastic outer shell and are stiffer. Bindings are the direct link between a rider's boots and the board. They come in a number of types and are designed to suit different boards and boot types.

THESE ARE A SOFT
BOOT (RIGHT) AND
A STRAP BINDING.
BOARDERS CAN
ALSO USE SPECIAL
STEP-IN BINDINGS
THAT ARE
QUICK AND
EASY TO
GET IN AND
OUT OF.

13

Science on the snow

You may not think it as you carve a turn, but science plays an important role in how you control your board. Flexibility and friction are key principles in the type of ride you'll get on the snow.

Plastic sandwich

Most snowboards consist of many layers. The core of the board is usually made of wood or high-density foam with metal inserts. Either side of the core are layers of plastic reinforced with fibreglass. These layers provide the board with its stiffness. The ability of a board to bend is called its flex. Beginner boards have more flex than racing boards, as flex makes a board slower but easier to ride.

THE LAYERS OF A BOARD ARE CLAMPED TOGETHER TIGHTLY AS THE GLUE DRIES.

Why wax?

Friction is the resistance created by two objects when they rub together. This rubbing-together force can slow movement down. The smoother the surfaces that rub together, the less friction is encountered. This is why snowboarders apply wax to the base of their boards. When applied with a special iron, wax forms an ultra-smooth coating over the base of the board. It allows the board to glide over the snow with less friction.

BOARDERS MELT BLOCKS OF SOLID WAX ONTO THE UNDERSIDE OF THEIR BOARDS USING A SPECIAL IRON.

On edge

The sides of a board, called the edges, are covered in a thin strip of metal. These metal edges dig into the snow when a boarder turns, increasing the grip and helping to change direction more easily.

AS A BOARDER DIGS IN THE EDGES, PLUMES OF SNOW ARE THROWN UP BEHIND.

BOARDING FACT

Snowboarding legend Tom Sims produced his first snowboard in a school class in the mid-1970s. His board consisted of a plank of wood with aluminium sheeting fitted to the bottom and a piece of carpet glued on top!

Basic moves

Although you can spend a lifetime perfecting moves and tricks, the basics of snowboarding are quick to pick up, especially if you start off with lessons from a certified snowboard instructor.

On board

Work out which stance most suits you – regular (left foot forwards) or goofy (right foot forwards). Either is fine, and there are pro boarders who use both stances. At first, try to skate around on a flat area to get the feel of the board. Put your front foot in its binding and push yourself gently along with your back foot.

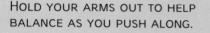

HOLD YOUR ARMS OUT TO HELP BALANCE AS YOU PUSH ALONG.

Turning

Leaning your body and moving your body weight are the key ways to get your snowboard to turn.

1. As you glide down the slope, keep your knees bent and your body relaxed. Start to lean slightly on your heels and turn your hips round in the direction you want to go. The board's nose will ease around into a heelside turn.

2. Take the pressure off your heels to stop the turn.

3. A frontside turn goes the other way to a heelside turn. You turn your hips and lean forwards slightly onto your toes to guide the board round in the opposite direction.

4. As you progress, you will be able to link these two types of turn together to zig-zag down a slope.

BOARDERS CAN CHANGE DIRECTION SMOOTHLY AND EASILY BY MOVING THEIR WEIGHT FROM THEIR HEELS TO THEIR TOES. THIS ACTION DIGS IN THE EDGES ON EITHER SIDE OF THE BOARD.

Jumps and slides

Once you've mastered the
basics, there are a
few other tricks
you can pick up.
These will open
up a whole range of stunts
that you can use on the slopes
to impress your friends.

Getting some air

The basic jump move in snowboarding is called
an Ollie. Get moving on a gentle slope and crouch
slightly on your board with your body
weight centred. Now bring your front
leg up firmly and transfer your weight
onto your back foot and the board's tail. Using the tail of
your board as a spring, pull your back foot up into the air.
With both knees drawn up to your chest, you and your
board will be off the ground and getting air. Try to get
the board level so that it is parallel with the ground
before you land. As you descend, straighten your legs
but keep your knees bent to act as shock absorbers.

USING AN OLLIE, A BOARDER
CAN GET AIR ON EVEN THE
FLATTEST OF SLOPES.

BOARDING FACT

Terje Haakensen scooped a prize of US$14,500 (£9000)
at the first ever indoor quarterpipe event to be held
in the USA. The 2000 Nike ACG Indoors featured
a monster 25-m high quarterpipe with artificial snow.

Sideslipping

One of the simplest ways of getting down a slope is sideslipping. At the end of each run, push the tail of your board downhill. You will slow and eventually stop. Then turn your upper body to face down the hill and the board will start to move back across the slope. At the other side of the slope, repeat the process. This move is also called falling leaf traversing, because the side-to-side path resembles a falling leaf.

A BOARDER ABOUT TO PERFORM A FRONTSIDE STOP.

WHETHER MOVING TO THE RIGHT OR TO THE LEFT, YOUR UPPER BODY IS ALWAYS FACING DOWN THE SLOPE DURING SIDESLIPPING.

Coming to a halt

A frontside stop begins with the same stance and move as the frontside turn on page 17. As you make a frontside turn, use your back foot to gradually ease and push the tail end of the board downhill. Your board's length will end up square to the slope. Your body and head will be facing uphill and you will coast to a halt.

Safe snowboarding

Snowboarding is fast and exciting, but it can also be dangerous. By following resort rules and by wearing the right equipment, you can still enjoy the thrills of boarding without too many of the risks.

Head protection

Helmets are important when learning snowboarding, when performing high-speed racing or when learning difficult new tricks. The snow can be hard or frozen solid and falling at high speed or from a great height will hurt. Helmets are lightweight, have vents to let air in and can be adjusted so that they fit firmly.

GOGGLES PROTECT THE EYES FROM THE SUN'S GLARE AND FROM SNOW SPRAYING OR DRIVING INTO YOUR FACE.

Snowboard sense

Winter resorts can be chaotic places, with hundreds of skiers and snowboarders of different skill levels all sharing the same slopes. Some resorts even have wardens who patrol the slopes and make sure that people are boarding and skiing safely, with consideration for others.

PLAN YOUR ROUTE DOWN AT THE TOP OF EACH RUN.

Snowboard rules

1 Learn about any specific resort rules – some resorts insist on boarders using safety leashes.

2 Stay alert for any obstacles, including overhanging branches.

3 If someone is slower and in front of you, it's your responsibility to get out of their way.

Bailing out

Snow doesn't always provide a nice, soft landing. Packed down snow can be hard, and there can also be patches of solid ice in some places. The most common injury in snowboarding is to the wrists. When you start to fall, try to roll into the fall and not stick your hands and arms out. This is called bailing out and helps spread the impact of the fall throughout your body.

BAILING OUT CAN BE PAINFUL IF NOT DONE PROPERLY.

BOARDING FACT

In 2001, Heikki Sorsa sailed 9.5 m above the lip of a quarterpipe to capture the big air world record.

Becoming a pro

Snowboarders improve their skills by spending as much time on their boards as possible, by seeking out new runs and by learning to ride in all sorts of conditions. Nailing new moves takes patience, bravery and persistence.

Fit to board

Snowboarding places huge demands on your body. You want to be in top shape to snowboard at your best, and a simple exercise regime can help you ride for longer. Stretching your back and leg muscles before boarding helps prevent injuries. Warming up also helps loosen your muscles and gets the blood pumping round your body.

BOARDERS SOMETIMES HAVE TO TRUDGE THROUGH THE SNOW TO REACH THE VERY BEST RUNS.

SNOWBOARDING TEAMS TRAVEL TO COMPETITIONS AND EVENTS ALL AROUND THE WORLD. HERE, MEMBERS OF THE VANS SNOWBOARDING TEAM POSE DURING A TRIP TO GRAND TARGHEE, WYOMING, USA.

Team spirit

Only a handful of snowboarders turn professional. Entering, winning and impressing at local competitions is a start, followed by doing the same in regional and national competitions. Snowboard companies may offer you free gear or pay for your entry fee and transport to a big competition. You may even qualify to join one of the pro teams that compete at events.

A PRO BOARDER SLIDES ALONG A JIB DURING A PHOTO SHOOT.

Films and photo shoots

Pro snowboarders don't just earn their money from races and events. Some have to take other jobs, working at winter resorts so that they can ride slopes in their free time. A few lucky pros are able to supplement their winnings by creating snowboarding films or by working on photo shoots for adverts and magazines.

BOARDING FACT

In 2003, Mammoth Mountain Snowboarding Park in California, USA, unveiled the world's largest snowboarding halfpipe. This monster, dubbed the Super-Duper Pipe, has 7-m-high walls and is a monstrous 200 m long.

Famous boarders

Snowboarding may be a young sport, but there are plenty of heroes, legends and superstars already. Over the years, these heroes have excelled in all disciplines including downhill racing and the high-flying halfpipe events.

Lesley McKenna

Originally starting out as a racer, British boarder Lesley McKenna enjoyed many top five World Cup finishes. She later moved on to the halfpipe. In this discipline, she qualified for the 2002 Olympics and went on to win the World Cup Halfpipe event in 2003.

Kelly Clark

An aggressive pipe rider who often gets over half a metre of air more than her opponents, American Kelly Clark had a fantastic year in 2002 when she won nearly every competition she entered. Riding slopestyle (see page 28) and quarterpipe, her greatest success came in halfpipe competitions where she won the US Open, gold medals at the Olympics and Winter X Games and double Grand Prix titles.

LESLEY MCKENNA HAS WON 19 TITLES IN VARIOUS SNOWBOARDING DISCIPLINES.

Victoria Jealouse

Victoria Jealouse is a backcountry (off-piste) boarding legend. A fearless mountain rider, this Californian is the star of many videos, including *The Prophecy* (2003).

Ross Powers

A halfpipe legend, blessed with power and incredible reactions, Ross Powers competed in his first US Open at the age of nine!

ROSS POWERS SOARS ABOVE A HALFPIPE.

BORN	Londonderry, Vermont, USA, 1979
HEIGHT	175 cm
WEIGHT	80 kg
CAREER HIGHLIGHTS	2003 US Open Halfpipe Champion, 2002 Olympic Gold Medallist, Gold Medallist at 2000 Gravity Games, Double gold medallist at 1998 Winter X Games.

The legend from Norway

Terje Haakonsen has been the most famous snowboarder on the planet for many years. Born in 1974 in the tiny village of Vinje in Norway, he started snowboarding at the age of 13. Haakonsen proved too hot a boarder for many of his peers. His fluid riding style and his creativity with tricks and moves have made him a legend. He's won both the US Open and the World Halfpipe Championships three times each and the European Halfpipe title five times.

TERJE HAAKONSEN WON HIS FIRST WORLD CHAMPIONSHIP AT THE AGE OF 17.

Around the globe

For beginner and intermediate snowboarders, there are no better places to head than the dedicated snowboard areas of winter resorts around the world.

Where to go

Slopes and snow are all snowboarders need to enjoy themselves. Some facilities even use artificial snow to create indoor slopes. But among the snowboarding community, certain places stand out as must-do locations, such as Chamonix in France.

South of the equator

Mount Buller near Melbourne is one of the most popular Australian resorts, while Thredbo Alpine Village is home to Australia's longest trail run for freeriders, measuring almost 6 km long.

A BOARDER LEAPS OVER ROCKS AT THE THREDBO ALPINE VILLAGE IN AUSTRALIA.

North America

The Whistler-Blackcomb region of Canada has long been a favourite with many pro and amateur snowboarders. Variety is the key, with over 230 marked runs, 12 alpine bowls, three halfpipes and two terrain parks. Jackson Hole in Wyoming, USA, is considered to be one of the premier steep freeriding resorts in the world.

GETTING AIR ABOVE THE SLOPES OF JAPAN.

A BOARDER NEGOTIATES A STEEP DESCENT AT JACKSON HOLE IN WYOMING.

The Far East

Japan was the site of the first Olympics to feature snowboarding at Nagano in 1998. Since then, the sport has boomed in this region of the world, with prime boarding spots at Shiga Kogen and Nozawa Onsen also in Japan.

BOARDING FACT

Snowboarding started out as a male sport but this changed fast. In 1989, there were nine boys for every girl snowboarder. Six years later, the ratio was three boys for every girl. At many resorts today, there are equal numbers of boy and girl boarders.

Great boarding

There are two main types of snowboarding competitions – racing events, such as the downhill, and freestyle events.

Spins and tricks

Freestyle events include big air, the halfpipe and slopestyle. In big air competitions, boarders launch off a ramp or hill and perform stunts in mid-air. Riders in freestyle events in halfpipes and quarterpipes are marked by teams of judges on style and the technical difficulty and accuracy of their moves. In slopestyle, competitors do their tricks while going down a hill, around obstacles and over bumps called moguls.

GETTING SOME AIR ABOVE THE SUPER-DUPER PIPE AT MAMMOTH PARKS, USA.

Olympics

LOCATION	Location varies every four years.
DESCRIPTION	Competitions over a number of events, including the halfpipe and giant slalom racing.
HISTORY	First included in the Winter Olympics in 1998 at Nagano, Japan.
ATTRACTIONS	Inclusion in the Olympics has boosted the sport's profile and has made celebrities out of many of the medallists, including Ross Powers, Nicola Thurst and Shannon Dunn.

PUTTING THE FINISHING TOUCHES TO AN ARTIFICIAL SNOW RAMP IN THE CENTRE OF INNSBRUCK, AUSTRIA.

Any time, any place

Snowboarding events are not just held at alpine resorts during the winter months. Thanks to artificial snow, huge ramps can be built in the middle of towns and cities anywhere in the world and at the height of summer! These spectacular freestyle events showcase some of the best boarders pulling amazing tricks. They have raised the profile of the sport and done much to increase its popularity.

Head to head

Most snowboard races are against the clock, but one event growing in popularity pits competitors against each other. Boardercross features four to six riders in a race down an obstacle course featuring jumps in a battle to be first across the line.

BOARDERCROSS EVENTS ARE DECIDED OVER A SERIES OF HEATS WITH THE FIRST TWO IN EACH RACE GOING ON TO THE NEXT ROUND. IN THE FINAL, THE FIRST PAST THE LINE WINS.

Boarding words

360 To spin round in a full circle in the air on the board.

airs Jumps on a snowboard, usually off a mogul, ramp or halfpipe.

avalanche Sudden fall of a large mass of snow and ice down a mountain.

bailing out A term used to describe crashing or falling to escape out of a trick.

boost A term used to describe catching air off a jump.

booter A large jump, bigger in size than a kicker.

bunny hill A gradual slope designed specifically for beginners.

carve To ride fast curves.

chatter Vibration of the board when riding over bumpy terrain.

corduroy Freshly groomed snow with finely ridged marks, like a giant rake has gone over its surface. Great for fast snowboarding.

drop or drop in To take your turn down a slope, jump or pipe.

fakie Riding the snowboard backwards from a normal stance.

goofy Riding with the right foot in front instead of the left foot, which is the normal stance.

grab Freestyle move where riders hold the tail or the nose of the board with their hands.

halfpipe A U-shaped bowl dug out of the snow for performing jumps and tricks.

heelside turn A turn made on the heelside edge.

jib A rail or anything other than snow that you can ride your board on.

kicker A medium-sized jump.

leash A safety device used to attach the snowboard to the front foot. This makes sure that the snowboard won't slide away while the boarder is getting in or out of the bindings.

ine The route or path chosen by a rider down a course.

ip trick Any trick performed on or near the top edge (the lip) of a halfpipe.

mogul A rounded bump in the middle of a course.

off piste Any place off a marked trail or run.

Ollie Pushing hard with your rear foot to jump off the ground.

pipe Another word for halfpipe.

piste A groomed area of snow prepared for snowboarders or skiers.

powder Deep dry snow – normally fresh snow that has just fallen.

stance How a boarder's feet are positioned on the snowboard.

twin tip A snowboard with an identically shaped nose and tail. This means that the board will ride equally well in either direction.

Films

Brainstorm (2002)
A collection of tricks and stunts with everything from huge urban rails to backcountry riding.
Vivid (2002)
One of the best snowboarding films released in recent years, it features awesome tricks and ultra-steep mountain descents.

Books to read

Snowboarding: The Essential Guide by Greg Goldman (New Holland, 2001)
Snowboarder's Start-up: Beginner's Guide to Snowboarding by Doug Werner, Jim Waide (Tracks Publishing, 1998)
Snowboarding Skills: The Back To Basic Essentials for All Levels by Cindy Kleh (Firefly Books, 2002)
The Illustrated Guide To Snowboarding by Kevin Ryan (Masters Press, 1999)
The Complete Snowboarder by Jeff Bennett, Scott Downey, Charles Arnell (Tabs Books, 2000)
Diary of a Snowboarding Freak by Paul Mason (Heinemann Library, 2003)
Pretty Good for a Girl: The Autobiography of a Snowboarding Pioneer by Tina Basich, Kathleen Gasperini (HarperEntertainment, 2003)

Magazines

White Lines magazine is the UK's leading snowboard magazine. *Onboard* magazine (www.onboardmag.com) is an online and print magazine dedicated to the European snowboarding scene. South of the equator, Australia has *Snowboarding* and *Australian Snowboarder* magazine, while New Zealand has *New Zealand Snowboarder*. Established way back in 1993, it is packed with features. Head to www.nzsnowboarder.nzl.com to order copies.

Index